Critical Thinking through Authentic Video

Expanding Horizons

CEFR A2-B1

世界を巡る映像で学ぶ総合英語〈準中級〉

Charles Browne　田邉祐司

NAN'UN-DO

映像
ストリーミング

ビデオ映像
無料視聴
のご案内

このテキストのビデオ映像を無料で視聴（ストリーミング）できます。
自習用としてご活用ください。
以下のサイトにアクセスしてテキスト番号で検索してください。

https://nanun-do.com　テキスト番号［**512086**］

※ 無線 LAN（WiFi）に接続してのご利用を推奨いたします。ストリーミング再生では、動画ファイルは保存されません。再生する度にデータをインターネット経由で読み込みますので、通信量にご注意ください。

※ キャリア回線を使用する場合、お使いのキャリアの料金プラン等によっては、高額なインターネット通信料金が発生する場合がありますのでご注意ください。

※ Expanding Horizons【CEFR A2-B1】映像視聴ページは以下のQR コードからもご利用になれます。

Foreword

Welcome to *Expanding Horizons: Critical Thinking through Authentic Video.*

It has long been known that one of the most important factors in developing English language skills over time is regular, daily exposure to input in English that is both at an appropriate level, as well as of personal interest to the learner. Expanding Horizons: Critical Thinking through Authentic Video is a 4-skill book that is designed to help you improve your English skills through exposure to authentic, award-winning videos that are carefully graded to follow the CEFR framework. The early units have videos, texts and activities that are at the A2+, while later units, are at the B1 level.

Although input is an essential starting point for language learning, it is not enough – regular, daily output, too, is crucial if you want to be able to advance beyond the beginner level. *Expanding Horizons* addresses this by taking a strong student-centered approach, which gives lots of opportunities for you to discuss and share your ideas, experiences and opinions with other students in English, using language in ways that will encourages the development of critical thinking skills. We have tried to strike a balance between fluency-oriented writing and pair/group activities (meaning you don't have to worry about making mistakes in English), and accuracy-focused shadowing, dictation/dictogloss and vocabulary development activities that will help improve your pronunciation, listening and speaking skills.

We believe that English language learning materials as well as the learning experience itself should be interesting, easy and fun and have done our best to make Expanding Horizons exactly that. We hope that you will enjoy studying English with this book and that it will help you to expand your horizons!

Dr. Charles Browne
Dr. Yuji Tanabe

Introduction to Activities in a Typical Unit:

1. **WARM UP: Talk about it**
   This activity is picture-based and designed to activate your real-world knowledge on the topic of the unit.

2. **VOCABULARY: Matching**
   This activity teaches the most important vocabulary words needed to understand the contents of the video. Definitions are given in easy English and match the meanings given in the video

3. **VIDEO: Before Watching**
   This activity usually asks you to make some predictions about what you think the video might be about. It helps draw you into the video as well as activate your knowledge on the topic.

4. **VIDEO: While Watching**
   There are several types of activities in this section, all of which can be characterized as "while-listening" activities, designed to help you to listen more actively and comprehend the video more fully.

5. **VIDEO: After Watching**
   These are more standard comprehension-style questions designed to make sure whether or not the students understood the key points of the video.

6. **DISCUSSION**
   This is a student-centered speaking activity designed to help you to think more deeply about the video, and to begin to communicate and share your ideas and opinions with others about this topic.

7. **WRITING: Critical Thinking**
   This activity is designed to help you to think more deeply about the topic as well as to move from an input-focus (the video and readings) to a more output-focus. This is done by asking you to write your ideas on the topic, which will also help you with the speaking activities later in the unit.

8. **QUOTABLE QUOTES**
   This picture-based activity introduces a quote, usually from a famous person, that is related to the topic of the unit. It is designed to help you to think deeply about the topic you have been studying.

9. **VOICE DICTION:** Video Shadowing

The dictation part of this activity gives you practice in developing your intensive listening skills while the shadowing part of the activity helps you to work on and improve your pronunciation, especially at the sentence level.

10. **CRITICAL DISCUSSION**

This activity builds on the writing activity given earlier in the unit, providing you with a real audience for your writing as well as a chance to discuss and think more critically about the topic at hand.

11. **WRITING**

This writing activity encourages you to share ideas as well as to help/teach each other the language needed to complete the activity. Like the previous writing activity, this one assumes your classmates will be the audience for the writing, which should help you to focus on writing in a way that will lead to fruitful/interesting discussions.

12. **OPTIONAL PROJECTS:** Individual and Group

Each unit provides at least 1-2 additional, optional projects should you want to extend the lesson or dig more deeply into the topic. Often the projects culminate with presenting the results to the class in the form of a PowerPoint, a poster or some kind of presentation, while encouraging the audience to actively ask follow-up questions.

Contents

Unit 1 **Holidays at Home** <Free Time> ······················ 9

Unit 2 **Soccer in Soweto** <Sports & Culture> ·············· 15

Unit 3 **Hannah's Van** <Life> ································ 21

Unit 4 **Bionic Boots** <Inventions> ························· 27

Unit 5 **Sophie's Costume** <Culture> ······················ 33

Unit 6 **Marvelous Mountain Biking** <Sports> ·········· 39

Unit 7 **A Family's History** <Family> ······················ 45

Unit 8 **Moai Heads** – The Pride of Rapa Nui <Free Time> • • • 51

Unit 9 **Shake My Beauty** <People> • 57

Unit 10 **Soul Food** <Food> • 63

Unit 11 **Super Street Art** <Art> • 69

Unit 12 **Two Very Different Brothers** <Family> • • • • • • • • • • 75

Unit 13 **A Cool Job** <Jobs> • 81

Unit 14 **How to Make Money and Travel Full-Time**
<Free Time> • 87

Unit 1

Holidays at Home

<Free Time>

Learning Goals	Vocabulary from the Video
Speaking Skills: ● **discussion** ● **planning** Writing Skills: ● **postcards**	Holidays Places in town

WARM UP: Talk about it

Work with a partner and answer the questions below.

1. Have you ever been to Paris?
2. Which tourist attractions would you like to visit there?

VOCABULARY: Matching

Match the words and phrases (1-8) and their definitions (a-h).

1. seaside	____	a. the coast, the seashore
2. tourist	____	b. an outdoor area where a fair is held
3. sight-seeing	____	c. a platform going from the shore into the sea
4. seafront	____	d. a tank of water where water creatures live
5. palace	____	e. the area by and around the sea; bay; beach
6. pier	____	f. an impressive building where a ruler lives
7. fairground	____	g. visiting places of interest
8. aquarium	____	h. a person who is traveling

VIDEO: Before Watching

Write 5 places tourists can visit in your town. Then compare your answers with a partner.

1. ______________________________
2. ______________________________
3. ______________________________
4. ______________________________
5. ______________________________

VIDEO: Sequencing

Activity 1:

Watch the video and order the places that Ellie visits on the map (1-7). The first one has been done for you.

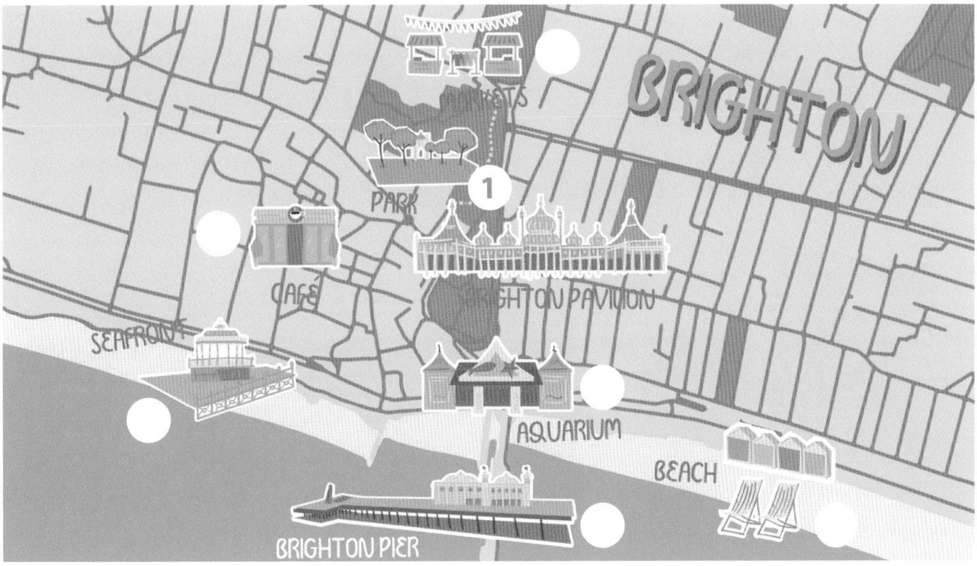

Activity 2:

1. Brighton is a famous British seaside ___town___.
2. Ellie takes a map, sun cream and ______________________.
3. At the shops Ellie buys ______________________.
4. Ellie enjoys a nice cup of ______________________.
5. At Brighton pier Ellie goes on a fairground ______________________.
6. Ellie has a traditional dinner of fish and ______________________ at the beach.

VIDEO: After Watching

Speaking

1. Imagine Ellie is coming to your hometown. What activities do you think she would enjoy? Work in groups and discuss.

2. Complete the table and then share your ideas with the rest of the class.

	Friday	Saturday	Sunday
Morning			
Afternoon			
Evening			

DISCUSSION

Make a small group and discuss the following questions.

1. What's the most interesting place you've ever visited?
2. If you could go anywhere in the world, where would you go? Why?

WRITING: Critical Thinking

Why do you think that so many people like to travel to new and exotic places? Write a short essay with your opinion and bring it to class next time.

QUOTABLE QUOTES: Warm up

"The real voyage of discovery consists not in seeking new landscapes, but in having new eyes."

By Marcel Proust

Look at the quote above. Think about this unit. What do you think the quote means?

VOICE DICTION: Video Shadowing

Start the video at 1:55 and play one sentence by Ellie.

1. Fill in the blank with the missing words.

   I'm so (   )! I love (   ) life.

2. Watch the scenes and pronounce at the same time. Repeat several times until you can do it smoothly.

CRITICAL DISCUSSION

Make groups of 3-4 students. Read each essay one by one. Then ...

- Choose the essay(s) with the most interesting ideas.
- Prepare to present those to the class in English.

WRITING

Now imagine you are Ellie. Write a postcard about her holiday in your town.

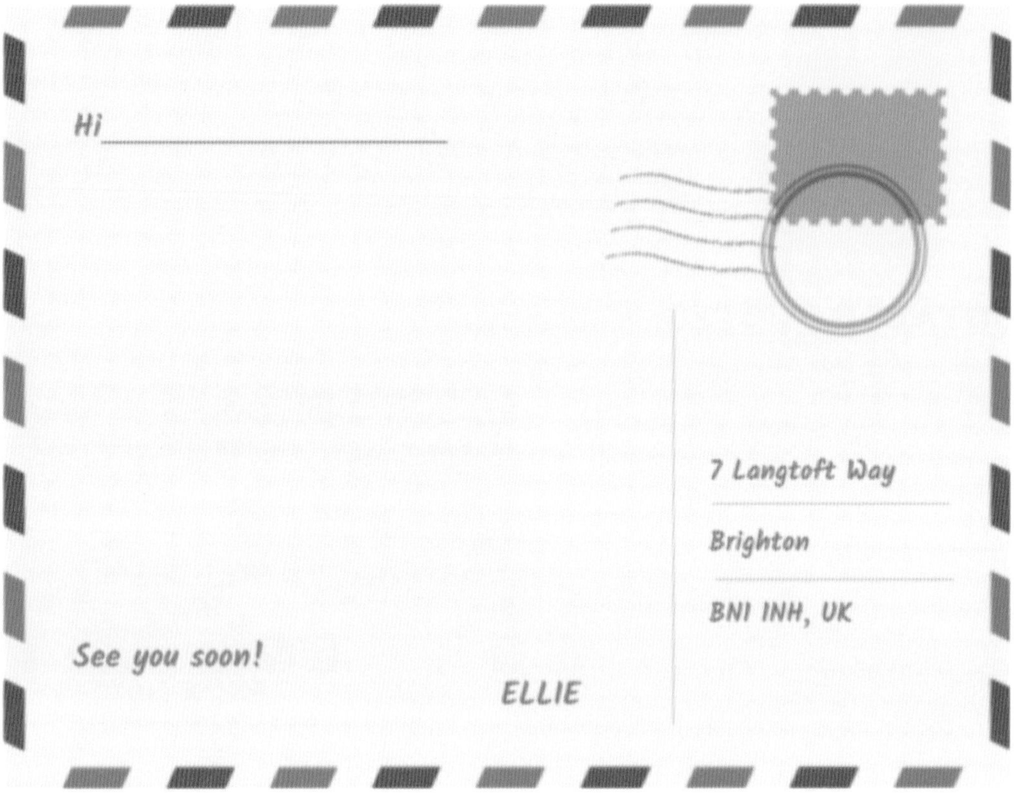

OPTIONAL PROJECTS: Individual and Group

Speaking

Show learners an example of a holiday brochure. Put them in small groups and have them research a holiday destination of their choice. They'll need to research the following information:

- Location
- Cost
- Festivals
- Other
- Population
- Landmarks
- Food
- Climate
- Attractions
- Transport

CEFR GOALS SELF- EVALUATION	
I can have a discussion in English with others.	1---2---3---4---5
I can work together to plan things with others.	1---2---3---4---5
I can understand the vocabulary of holiday(s).	1---2---3---4---5
I can understand the vocabulary of places in town.	1---2---3---4---5

Unit 2
Soccer in Soweto
<Sports & Culture>

Learning Goals	Vocabulary from the Video
Speaking Skills: ● **discussion** ● **comparing pictures** Writing Skills: ● **a letter**	Football Sounds and Music

WARM UP: Talk about it

Work with a partner and answer the questions below.

1. Have you ever been to or watched a soccer game?
2. Which famous players or teams do you like best?

VOCABULARY: Matching

Match the words and phrases (1-8) and their definitions (a-h).

1. vuvuzelas	____	a. an entertaining performance for other people
2. stadium	____	b. a skillful act done for entertainment
3. match	____	c. the winner of a contest
4. half-time	____	d. a loud sound
5. tricks	____	e. a place where professional sports are played
6. noise	____	f. a sports contest between two teams
7. show	____	g. a long horn blown by fans in South Africa
8. champion	____	h. a break taken when half the game is completed

VIDEO: Before Watching

1. Complete the sentence.

   I enjoy watching ______________________________.

2. Walk around the class and find other people who like watching the same sport as you.

VIDEO: While Watching

Activity 1:

Watch the video and complete the sentence.

Young people in Soweto love football and ______________________________.

Activity 2:

Watch the video again and circle true (T) or false (F).

1	**Soccer City is the biggest football stadium in Africa.**	**T**	**F**
2	**South Africa won the World Cup in 2010.**	**T**	**F**
3	**The fans play musical instruments to make a lot of noise.**	**T**	**F**
4	**People sit down and watch the match quietly.**	**T**	**F**
5	**Dan Magness is a famous British footballer.**	**T**	**F**
6	**In Soweto, freestyle is similar to dancing.**	**T**	**F**
7	**At school, children sing and dance before playing football.**	**T**	**F**

VIDEO: After Watching

Speaking

a. Which parts of the body to the freestylers use? Write or draw.

HEAD

b. Discuss your favorite tricks. Use these words to help ...

- I like the trick he does with his ...
- He goes like this! (use gestures to help you describe the trick)

DISCUSSION

Make a small group and discuss the following questions.

1. Are there other sports you like watching tricks in?
2. Use the internet to find videos you like and show to your group.
3. Discuss the trick videos, choose the best one, then present to another group or to the class.

WRITING: Critical Thinking

Which athlete most inspires or excites you? Why? Write a short essay with your opinion and bring it to class next time.

QUOTABLE QUOTES:

"I never tried to hide the fact that my only goal is to be the best."

By Cristiano Ronaldo

Look at the quote above. Think about this unit. What do you think the quote means?

VOICE DICTION: Video Shadowing

Start the video at 1:25 and play two sentences by Dan.

1. Fill in the blank with the missing words.

   I've just performed a nearly (   ) show in front of (   ) 90,000 people. What a (   )!

2. Watch the scenes and pronounce at the same time. Repeat several times until you can do it smoothly.

CRITICAL DISCUSSION

Make groups of 3-4 students. Read each essay one by one. Then ...

- Choose the essay(s) with the most interesting ideas.
- Prepare to present those to the class in English.

WRITING

Read the fact file about Dan from the video.

<table>
<tr><td colspan="2">Name
DAN MAGNESS</td></tr>
<tr><td>Sport
Football Freestyle</td><td rowspan="4">
</td></tr>
<tr><td>Age
35</td></tr>
<tr><td>Nationality
British</td></tr>
<tr><td>Hometown
Guildford, UK</td></tr>
<tr><td>Achievements and trophies
He was the first person to keep a football in the air for 24 hours.
He walked for 11 days while kicking a football up in the air from London to Manchester!</td><td>Other information
He is now a TV presenter. He does tricks at lots of sports events.</td></tr>
</table>

Choose a famous sports star. Find Information, then complete the fact file. When you are finished, display your fact file for other students to read.

<table>
<tr><td colspan="2">Name</td></tr>
<tr><td>Sport</td><td rowspan="4"></td></tr>
<tr><td>Age</td></tr>
<tr><td>Nationality</td></tr>
<tr><td>Hometown</td></tr>
<tr><td>Achievements and trophies</td><td>Other information</td></tr>
</table>

OPTIONAL PROJECTS: Individual and Group

Work in small groups and research about the sport of soccer in Japan, for example Japan's performance in the Olympics, World Cup, or top men's and women's teams. Each group choose a different topic and begin to gather data and pictures. Then work collaboratively to make a poster containing the information and use it to give a 2-minute presentation to the rest of the class.

CEFR GOALS SELF- EVALUATION	
I can have discussions in English.	1---2---3---4---5
I can create compare pictures in English.	1---2---3---4---5
I can understand the vocabulary of football.	1---2---3---4---5
I can understand the vocabulary of sounds and music.	1---2---3---4---5
I can talk about Japanese soccer.	1---2---3---4---5

Unit 3
Hannah's Van
<Life>

Learning Goals	Vocabulary from the Video
Speaking Skills: • **discussion** Writing Skills: • **an article**	At home Free time activities

WARM UP: Talk about it

RVs (recreational vehicles) are very comfortable to ride in. They are a very popular way to travel across America and can be rented almost anywhere.

Work with a partner and answer the questions below.

1. Have you ever been in or seen an RV before? What did you think?
2. Would you like to travel in an RV someday? Why or why not?

VOCABULARY: Matching

Match the words and phrases (1-8) and their definitions (a-h).

1. rent	____	a. a small space that can be lived in
2. stuff	____	b. to visit a place used for physical activity
3. shelf	____	c. various things a person has
4. room	____	d. payment made for use of land or living space
5. to get out	____	e. to go up a wall or cliff using your hands and feet
6. go to the gym	____	f. a flat piece of wood on a wall for books and things
7. do yoga	____	g. to go out to different places
8. go climbing	____	h. relaxing physical and mental activity from India

VIDEO: Before Watching

Work with a partner.

1. Imagine you are going to start living in a van. Search the internet for pictures and information on a van you would like to live in. Prepare reasons for your choice.
2. Compare your van with choices made by other pairs.

VIDEO: While Watching

Activity 1:

Check off all the items you hear:

bed　beach　bathroom　chair　gym　table　telephone

Activity 2:

Answer the following questions:

1. Why did Hannah move to her van?
2. When does Hannah do yoga outside?
3. What is Hannah's favorite thing in the van?
4. Where does Hannah shower?
5. What are Hannah's hobbies?
6. What is the best thing about being in the van?

VIDEO: After Watching

Natural Speech

1. Watch the video from 1:04-1:28 again. Write down all the words you can hear Hannah say clearly.

2. Now, make pairs and compare your answers. Try to use them to make complete sentences for what you think Hannah said.
3. Listen again with captions on to check your answers.
4. Practice saying Hannah's sentences in small groups, being careful to use the correct word and sentence stress. Your teacher will help you.

DISCUSSION

Make a small group and discuss the following questions.

1. Have you ever gone camping or done something where you had to live more simply than normal? What challenges did you face?
2. Do you think you could do what Hannah did while going to college? Why or why not?

WRITING: Critical Thinking

Living on your own and going to university can be very expensive. Think about some creative ways a person could cut costs and save money. Then write a short essay introducing some of these ideas.

QUOTABLE QUOTES:

"Not all who wander are lost."

By J.R.R. Tolkien

Look at the quote above. Think about this unit. What do you think the quote means?

VOICE DICTION: Video Shadowing

Start the video at 2:11 and play.

1. Fill in the blank with the missing words.

   The best thing about being in the (   ) actually is if you're being very (   ) you can reach everything and (   ) from being in bed.

2. Watch the scene and pronounce at the same time. Repeat several times until you can do it smoothly.

CRITICAL DISCUSSION

Make groups of 3-4 students. Read each essay one by one. Then ...

- Choose the essay(s) with the most interesting ideas.
- Prepare to present those to the class in English.

WRITING

Even with such a small living space, Hannah was able to do exercise regularly. Work in a small group and think of as many ideas as possible on "how to stay fit in a small space". After you have generated 4-5 ideas, work individually to write a short essay on this topic.

OPTIONAL PROJECTS: Individual and Group

Work in small groups and try to design a device what saves space, like Hannah's shoe rack. After you are finished, prepare a sales presentation to the rest of the class. The class will then vote on which products should be invested in. Be creative!

CEFR GOALS SELF- EVALUATION	
I can have discussions in English.	1---2---3---4---5
I can write an article in English.	1---2---3---4---5
I can understand the vocabulary of homes.	1---2---3---4---5
I can understand the vocabulary of free time activities.	1---2---3---4---5
I can make a sales pitch.	1---2---3---4---5

Unit 4
Bionic Boots
<Inventions>

Learning Goals	Vocabulary from the Video
Speaking Skills: ● **discussing inventions** Writing Skills: ● **imagining superpowers**	Words related to sports Action/movement verbs

WARM UP: Talk about it

Work with a partner and answer the questions below.

1. What is the most unusual invention you have heard about or seen?
2. What invention would you like to see made in the future?

VOCABULARY: Matching

Match the words and phrases (1-8) and their definitions (a-h).

1. boots	____	a. a competition to try to be first or the fastest
2. race	____	b. something with 2 wheels moved by turning 2 pedals
3. move	____	c. to be in a state of motion
4. bicycle	____	d. an amazing power normal humans don't have
5. to make	____	e. a type of shoe that covers the foot and lower leg
6. to run	____	f. an activity that uses mental energy
7. to work	____	g. to create or produce something
8. superpower	____	h. to move faster than walking by taking quick steps

VIDEO: Before Watching

Work with a partner. If you could have one superpower, what would it be? Write down your ideas below and then share with the class.

VIDEO: While Watching

Activity 1:

Watch the video and answer the question.

Do you think that the technology in this video will change the way we travel in the future? Why or why not? Share your ideas with the class and then vote.

Activity 2:

Read the sentences and guess which order they appear in the video. Watch the video again and check your answers.

	It's a lot harder than it looks, but Bionic Boots might just be the future of how we move.
	Justin has gone to San Francisco to meet Keahi. Keahi has made special boots that could make people into superheroes.
	He thinks his Bionic Boots are better than bicycles because they are faster, and easier to carry around.
	Keahi has done lots of work to make special shoes that make him run like an animal, but he's always trying to improve them.

VIDEO: After Watching

Natural Speech

1. Watch the video from 0:50-1:10 again. Write down all the words you can hear the narrator say clearly.

2. Now, make pairs and compare your answers. Try to use them to make complete sentences for what you think the narrator said.
3. Listen again with captions on to check your answers.
4. Practice saying the narrator's sentences in small groups, being careful to use the correct word and sentence stress. Your teacher will help you.

DISCUSSION

Make a group and discuss the following questions:

1. Would you use Bionic Boots instead of a bicycle? Why or why not?
2. Beyond Bionic Boots, what other things do you think we might be able to do with our bodies in the future?

WRITING: Critical Thinking

Inventions can change the course of our lives. Think about some of the important inventions of the past 100 year and how they have affected us. Discuss this topic with a partner, then write a short essay introducing some of these ideas.

Bonus Activity: write a few sentences describing the invention you chose without mentioning it by name. Then read them out loud to other groups and see if they can guess your invention.

QUOTABLE QUOTES:

"To invent, you need a good imagination and a pile of junk."

By Thomas A. Edison

Look at the quote above. Think about this unit. What do you think the quote means?

VOICE DICTION: Video Shadowing

Start the video at 0:44 and play

1. Fill in the blank with the missing words.

   Thank you very much for inviting me to your (   ) of (   ) science.

2. Watch the scene and pronounce at the same time. Repeat several times until you can do it smoothly.

CRITICAL DISCUSSION

Make groups of 3-4 students. Read each essay one by one. Then ...

- Choose the essay(s) with the most interesting ideas.
- Prepare to present those to the class in English.

WRITING

If you could invent one thing that would make your life easier, what would it be? Work in a small group and think of as many ideas as possible. After you have generated 4-5 ideas, work individually to write a short essay on this topic.

OPTIONAL PROJECTS: Individual and Group

Imagine you have been given the job of marketing and selling Keahi's boots. Work together in small groups to create an advertising campaign for the books. You should consider the following points:

- Who the target market is
- Where you will sell the boots
- How much the boots will cost
- How/where you will advertise the boots
- Will there be any warnings or age restrictions on the boots?

Each group then presents their ideas to the class and takes questions.

CEFR GOALS SELF- EVALUATION	
I can discuss inventions in English.	1---2---3---4---5
I can talk about imaginary superpowers.	1---2---3---4---5
I can understand the vocabulary related to sports.	1---2---3---4---5
I can understand how to use action/movement verbs.	1---2---3---4---5
I can research and talk about marketing a product.	1---2---3---4---5

Unit 5
Sophie's Costume
<Culture>

Learning Goals	Vocabulary from the Video
Speaking Skills: ● **describing a hobby** Writing Skills: ● **life skills from hobbies**	Words related to art and media Words related to learning something

WARM UP: Talk about it
Work with a partner and answer the questions below.

1. What do you know about Japanese anime and cartoons?
2. Have you ever seen or know about cosplay?

VOCABULARY: Matching

Match the words and phrases (1-8) and their definitions (a-h).

1. cosplay	____	a. to develop a skill to do something new
2. design	____	b. a special kind of clothes to look like someone else
3. costume	____	c. to succeed or do successfully
4. outfit	____	d. dressing up as a character from a film, book or game
5. learn how to	____	e. a set of clothes worn together
6. try again	____	f. to make a mistake in the process of learning
7. learn the hard way	____	g. to do something again in order to succeed
8. to work	____	h. to plan or create something

VIDEO: Before Watching

The "Who am I" game?

1. Write down the name of two comic book or pop culture figures on small pieces of paper.
2. Make a small group. Each person chooses a piece of paper, making it visible so the rest of the group can see.
3. Each person takes turns asking the group yes/no questions, trying to guess who the person is. Whoever guesses first is the winner.

VIDEO: While Watching

Activity 1:

Watch the video and put the steps of the cosplay project into the right order.

take pictures	make a video	design the costume
do cosplay	build/make the costume	dress up

Activity 2:

The second time you watch the video, decide whether the following statements are true or false.

	TRUE	FALSE
Sophie makes a cosplay outfit every year.		
People usually make their costumes in a day or two.		
Sophie thinks you can learn many useful skills from cosplay.		
She used her costume only once.		
Sophie took part in a costume contest, but didn't win.		
She made new friends with similar interests to hers.		

VIDEO: After Watching

Think about the different skills that Sophie had to learn during her project. Arrange the skills along the chart according to the type of skill and your personal interest in developing each skill.

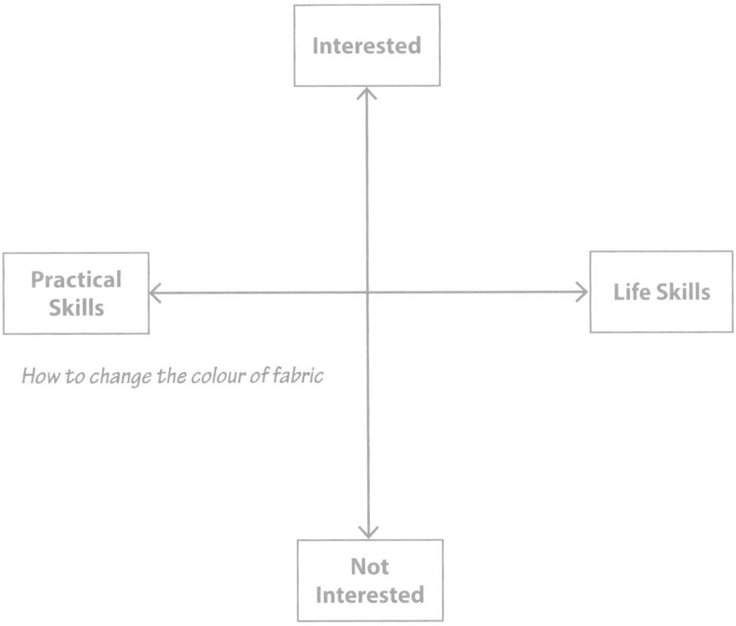

DISCUSSION

Make a group and discuss the following questions:

1. Which cartoon characters have been made into movies?
2. Which cartoon characters do you think have had the most influence on popular culture? Why?

WRITING: Critical Thinking

What life skills can a hobby teach us? You can refer to Sophie's hobby or one of your own. Discuss this topic with a partner, then write a short essay introducing some of these ideas.

QUOTABLE QUOTES:

"Clothes make a statement. Costumes tell a story."

By Mason Cooley

Look at the quote above. Think about this unit. What do you think the quote means?

VOICE DICTION: Video Shadowing

Start the video at 0:46 and play

1. Fill in the blank with the missing words.

   One of the (   ) that I realized I (   ) cosplay is that it kind of (   ) learn new skills all the time.

2. Watch the scene and pronounce at the same time. Repeat several times until you can do it smoothly.

CRITICAL DISCUSSION

Make groups of 3-4 students. Read each essay one by one. Then ...

- Choose the essay(s) with the most interesting ideas.
- Prepare to present those to the class in English.

WRITING

Create a poster about your favorite comic or pop culture figure. Each poster should contain: 1) an image of the figure made in mixed techniques and materials, such as paint and fabrics, drawings, collages, etc. and 2) a profile of the figure with bio, preferences, etc. The posters will then be exhibited in a public place (like a school hall or on the walls around the classroom). During the opening ceremony, the artists have to answer questions about their chosen figures.

OPTIONAL PROJECTS: Individual and Group

Working as a group, research cosplay and agree on a favorite comic or pop culture figure of whom to make a costume. Work together to make the costume, documenting the process (creative solutions, know-how, etc.) using simple language in a series of video/audio/blog entries. Finally, organise a costume contest in which you announce each figure, the elements of its costume and materials in English.

CEFR GOALS SELF- EVALUATION	
I can discuss describe a hobby in English.	1---2---3---4---5
I can write about life skills learned from hobbies.	1---2---3---4---5
I can understand words related to art and media.	1---2---3---4---5
I can understand words related to learning something.	1---2---3---4---5

Unit 6
Marvelous Mountain Biking <Sports>

Learning Goals	Vocabulary from the Video
Speaking Skills: ● **an interview** Writing Skills: ● **a brochure**	Sports Challenges

WARM UP: Talk about it

Work with a partner and answer the questions below.

1. Do you like biking?
2. What do you know/like about mountain biking?
3. Tell about your favorite bike or bike experience, or a “dream” bike experience.

VOCABULARY: Matching

Match the words and phrases (1-8) and their definitions (a-h).

1. athlete	____	a. involving the chance for hurt or damage; risky
2. sports competition	____	b. a contest to find the best athlete or team
3. climb	____	c. a person using a bicycle
4. cyclist	____	d. a person who is very good at a certain sport
5. freezing	____	e. an unplanned event that causes damage
6. accident	____	f. when the temperature is very cold
7. tough	____	g. when a cyclist rides up a difficult mountain
8. dangerous	____	h. difficult to do or deal with

VIDEO: Before Watching

Look at these dangers. Think of a sport for each one and explain why it is dangerous.

Getting injured	Being too hot	Being too cold	Falling
Football, because you could break a leg if another player tackles you hard.			

VIDEO: While Watching

Activity 1:

Work with a partner. You will watch a video about a very difficult bike race in the Himalayas. What difficulties do you think you will hear about? Watch and check your ideas.

Activity 2:

a. Watch the video again and put the following numbers in the order that you hear them in the video.

Order	Numbers from Video	This number refers to ...
	10	
	5500	
	-10	
	35	
	4500	
1	400	**Distance of the race in km.**

b. Can you remember what the numbers refer to? Write your answers above and then watch the video or read the transcript to check.

VIDEO: After Watching

Speaking

a. Work in pairs. Write down 3 questions you would like to ask Richard.

Example:
"How did you feel when you finished the race?"

b. Now take turns to imagine you are Richard and answer the questions. Then try again with another pair.

DISCUSSION

Make a small group and discuss the following questions.

1. Have you ever been in a race?
2. What kind of preparations did you make for it?
3. How did it feel before, during and after the race?

WRITING: Critical Thinking

Why do you think so many people like dangerous sports like extreme mountain biking? What is the appeal? Write a short essay with your opinion and bring it to class next time.

QUOTABLE QUOTES:

"A bicycle ride around the world begins with a single pedal stroke."

By Scott Stoll, a Professor who travelled around the world on his bicycle

Look at the quote above. Think about this unit. What do you think the quote means?

VOICE DICTION: Video Shadowing

Start the video at 1:21 and play one sentence by the narrator.

1. Fill in the blank with the missing words.

   There are many (   ) for the (   ).

2. Watch the scenes and pronounce at the same time. Repeat several times until you can do it smoothly.

CRITICAL DISCUSSION

Make groups of 3-4 students. Read each essay one by one. Then ...

- Choose the essay(s) with the most interesting ideas.
- Prepare to present those to the class in English.

WRITING

a. Work in groups. You are going to write a brochure about a local sporting event. Choose the sporting event together.

b. Decide who will research each section. You may want to include:
   - Logistics: what, when, where, how much it costs, etc.
   - Why people like it: What people get out of it, what type of people attend, etc.
   - Difficulties: dangers, recommendations, etc.

c. When you've finished, review the brochure with your group and make any corrections necessary.

d. Now display your brochure for other classmates to see. Vote on which team has the best brochure.

OPTIONAL PROJECTS: Individual and Group

Work in a group and research the benefits of exercising and the drawbacks of overexercising. Then work collaboratively to make a poster containing the information and use it to give a 2-minute presentation to the rest of the class.

CEFR GOALS SELF- EVALUATION	
I can interview others.	1---2---3---4---5
I can create a travel brochure.	1---2---3---4---5
I can understand the vocabulary of athletics.	1---2---3---4---5
I can understand the vocabulary of challenges.	1---2---3---4---5
I can discuss about biking and mountain.	1---2---3---4---5

Unit 7
A Family's History
<Family>

Learning Goals	Vocabulary from the Video
Speaking Skills: • **discussing family history** Writing Skills: • **questions and answers**	Words related to family adjectives

WARM UP: Talk about it

Work with a partner and answer the questions below.

1. How many generations of relatives have you met (Grandparents? Great grandparents?)?
2. How far back do you know your family's history? Where are they from?

VOCABULARY: Matching

Match the words and phrases (1-8) and their definitions (a-h).

1. ancestors	____	a. any person you are related to
2. relatives	____	b. to be greatly surprised
3. family tree	____	c. a family member from a long time ago
4. great-grandfather	____	d. to be known by many people
5. amazed	____	e. the father of your grandfather or grandmother
6. exciting	____	f. to have great power or strength
7. famous	____	g. a chart that shows the relation of family members
8. powerful	____	h. to cause enthusiasm or eagerness

VIDEO: Before Watching

How many different kinds of family members can you think of? Write them below.

- grandfather	-
-	-
-	-
-	-
-	-
-	-

VIDEO: While Watching

Activity 1:

Watch the video and answer the question.

What is surprising about Danny's family history?

Activity 2:

Watch the video again and correct the sentences.

Ex. First Danny goes to a ~~museum~~ to find information on his family.
library

1. An expert shows Danny a map of the world.

2. He learns that six hundred years ago his family were very rich.

3. Lord Tollemache and Danny are father and son.

4. Danny finds out he is related to King Henry the first.

5. Danny says his life will be very different from now.

VIDEO: After Watching

Speaking

1. Draw your family tree:

2. In small groups ask each other questions about your family trees. Use these words to help:
   - Who is this?
   - What is he/she like?
   - He/She is ... kind/brave/intelligent.

WRITING

1. With a partner, write 5 questions Danny could ask King Edward III.

2. Swap your questions with another group. Imagine you are King Edward III and answer the questions. Write down your answers.

3. Swap back your questions and read the answers. Correct any mistakes you notice.

DISCUSSION

Make a small group and discuss the following questions.

1. Do you or any of your friends have a famous relative?
2. Do you think having a famous relative would affect you in some way?

WRITING: Critical Thinking

Some people are becoming more interested in family history research. Others argue we should focus on the present and future generation. Discuss this topic with a partner, then write a short essay introducing some of these ideas.

QUOTABLE QUOTES:

"There are only two lasting things we can give to our children — one is roots, and the other, wings."

By Hodding S. Carter

Look at the quote above. Think about this unit. What do you think the quote means?

VOICE DICTION: Video Shadowing

Start the video at 0:42 and play.

1. Fill in the blank with the missing words.

   He learns about his (   ). She was poor (   ) had a hard (   ).

2. Watch the scenes and pronounce at the same time. Repeat several times until you can do it smoothly.

CRITICAL DISCUSSION

Make groups of 3-4 students. Read each essay one by one. Then ...

- Choose the essay(s) with the most interesting ideas.
- Prepare to present those to the class in English.

WRITING

Imagine you are one of your great-great-great grand-children, far in the future, writing about your present self. Write about an event from your own history from that perspective. Then share your essay with other students. Read other student's essays and write questions and comments to help them to improve their essay. When you get your essay back, rewrite it to address the questions others ask you.

OPTIONAL PROJECTS: Individual and Group

Work in small groups and research a royal family of your choice. You can choose any era and any country. After you are finished, prepare a poster to show the rest of the class. Include a small family tree with dates of birth/death and a short biography of one of the members. Try to answer some of the following questions:

- Who were they?
- Where did they live?
- What are they famous for?
- If they are from another era, how did they die?

CEFR GOALS SELF- EVALUATION	
I can discuss family histories in English.	1---2---3---4---5
I can ask and answer questions about family histories.	1---2---3---4---5
I can understand the vocabulary related to families.	1---2---3---4---5
I can understand how to use adjectives.	1---2---3---4---5
I can research family history.	1---2---3---4---5

Unit 8

Moai Heads – The Pride of Rapa Nui <Travel>

Learning Goals	Vocabulary from the Video
Speaking Skills: • **discussing travel** Writing Skills: • **emails**	Words related to travel Adjectives

WARM UP: Talk about it

Work with a partner and answer the questions below.

1. What is the oldest famous structure you've ever visited?
2. What did you like about it?

VOCABULARY: Matching

Match the words and phrases (1-8) and their definitions (a-h).

1. hard to reach ____ a. being the only one of its kind
2. location ____ b. very large
3. icon ____ c. something or someone known by many people
4. recognize ____ d. something that is a symbol worthy of knowing
5. well-known ____ e. the place where something is
6. spectacular ____ f. a place that is difficult to get to
7. unique ____ g. beautiful in an amazing or dramatic way
8. sheer ____ h. to identify something you have seen before

VIDEO: Before Watching

Work in small groups. For each picture, try to guess the key information about it. Check your answers with another group then confirm your answers with the teacher.

Name of icon	Where it is located	How old it is

VIDEO: While Watching

Activity 1:

Watch the video. Then work with a partner to decide the best title for the video. Compare your answer with other pairs, giving reasons for your choice.

1. The adventures of Te Radar
2. The Moai heads of Rapa Nui
3. A 1990's film mystery

Activity 2:

Answer the following questions while watching the video. Then compare your answers with a partner.

1. Where is Papa Nui?
2. How far has Te Radar travelled to get to Papa Nui?
3. How many Moai heads are there on the island?
4. Why were the Moai heads made?
5. We can only see the Moai heads. Where are the bodies and how long are they?
6. Why is there a Moai under the sea?

VIDEO: After Watching

Natural Speech

1. Watch the video from 0:41-0:49 again. Write down all the words you can hear the narrator say clearly.
2. Now, make pairs and compare your answers. Try to use them to make complete sentences for what you think the narrator said.
3. Listen again with captions on to check your answers.
4. Practice saying Te's sentences in small groups, being careful to use the correct word and sentence stress. Your teacher will help you.
5. Te uses the expression "there's something about ...", which means: someone or something that has a particular quality but you are not certain what it is. Try to come up with your own sentences using the same expression and practice using them with each other.

DISCUSSION

Re-watch the section of video 2:06-2:28. As stated in the video, no one really knows how these huge statues were made or moved into position.

Make a group and discuss this mystery. Try to come up with a few possible explanations and then present your ideas to the class.

WRITING: Critical Thinking

How can travelling to historical places help us to learn and grow. Discuss this topic with a partner, then write a short essay introducing some of these ideas.

QUOTABLE QUOTES:

"The world is a book and those who do not travel read only a page."

By St. Augustine

Look at the quote above. Think about this unit. What do you think the quote means?

VOICE DICTION: Video Shadowing

Start the video at 1:23 and play

1. Fill in the blank with the missing words.

   This is only the ( ). If you could imagine the ( ) underneath, it's buried. It is probably seven or eight meters ( ).

2. Watch the scene and pronounce at the same time. Repeat several times until you can do it smoothly.

CRITICAL DISCUSSION

Make groups of 3-4 students. Read each essay one by one. Then ...

- Choose the essay(s) with the most interesting ideas.
- Prepare to present those to the class in English.

WRITING

Imagine you just returned from visiting Easter Island. Write an email to a friend describing the trip and the Moai heads. Use the events in the video as a guide.

OPTIONAL PROJECTS: Individual and Group

Working in small groups, choose and research an icon of the world. Then work together to produce a flyer based on your research. The flyer should cover all of the key information on the icon and present it in a way that can be easily understood.

CEFR GOALS SELF- EVALUATION	
I can discuss travel in English.	1---2---3---4---5
I can write an email describing a travel experience.	1---2---3---4---5
I can understand words related to travel.	1---2---3---4---5
I can understand and use adjectives.	1---2---3---4---5

Unit 9
Shake My Beauty
<People>

Learning Goals	Vocabulary from the Video
Speaking Skills: • **discussing beauty** Writing Skills: • **emailing advice**	Words related to appearance Adjectives related to feelings

WARM UP: Talk about it

Work with a partner and answer the questions below.

1. Which well-known men and women do you find attractive?
2. What specific things do you like about their looks?

VOCABULARY: Matching

Match the words and phrases (1-8) and their definitions (a-h).

1. overwhelmed	____	a. things that make something less than perfect
2. embarrassed	____	b. to be strongly affected at an emotional level
3. feel like	____	c. not attractive or un-appealing
4. makeup	____	d. to seem to be like something
5. foundation	____	e. things which are put on your face to improve appearance
6. acne	____	f. a base layer of makeup put on your face
7. gross	____	g. a skin condition, usually appearing on your face
8. imperfections	____	h. to cause someone to feel ashamed

VIDEO: Before Watching

Work in pairs and try to answer the following questions:

1. What is beauty?
2. What is the definition of beauty?

VIDEO: While Watching

Activity 1:

Think about the following question while watching the video:

"Do you think Hayley is happier now than when she was before?"

Activity 2:

Watch the video. Make notes on the context these words were used in the video. Check and discuss your answers with a partner, then check using the video transcript or by watching the video again with captions on.

Cover	
House	
Pretty	
Embarrased	
Help	

VIDEO: After Watching

Watch the video again and complete the sentences with the information from the video.

Hayley felt overwhelmed when ...

Hayley felt gross when ...

Hayley got a lot of hate when ...

DISCUSSION

Make a small group and divide into 2 teams. Debate the question: Do you think social media makes people feel better or worse about their appearance? Each team positions themselves either for or against. After the debate is over, discuss the topic and present your opinion to the class.

WRITING: Critical Thinking

Using Hayley's experience overcoming acne, write a pen pal email to a student who is struggling with body insecurity. Suggest ideas to help them gain confidence, and think of a creative outlet where they can express.

QUOTABLE QUOTES:

"Being liked for the way you looked is worse than not being liked at all."

By Amanda Hocking, author

Look at the quote above. Think about this unit. What do you think the quote means?

VOICE DICTION: Video Shadowing

Start the video at 0:17 and play.

1. Fill in the blank with the missing words.

   I decided to (   ) foundation. It was only (   ) me, and I felt like I wasn't (   ).

2. Watch the scene and pronounce at the same time. Repeat several times until you can do it smoothly.

CRITICAL DISCUSSION

Make groups of 3-4 students. Read each essay one by one. Then ...

- Choose the essay(s) with the most interesting ideas.
- Prepare to present those to the class in English.

WRITING

Design and write a short anti-bullying advertisement which supports people's imperfections. Look on the internet to help you get ideas. Then display all the advertisements and the class votes on which one they find most powerful.

OPTIONAL PROJECTS: Individual and Group

Work in small groups. Each group should work together to create a health awareness poster to educate teenagers about a common health problem for teenagers like acne. Research the causes and effects, treatments, etc. and create a poster with information and diagrams about the chosen health problem.

CEFR GOALS SELF- EVALUATION	
I can discuss the topic of beauty in English.	1---2---3---4---5
I can write an email giving advice.	1---2---3---4---5
I can understand words related to appearance.	1---2---3---4---5
I can understand and use adjectives related to feelings.	1---2---3---4---5

Unit 10
Soul Food <Food>

Learning Goals	Vocabulary from the Video
Speaking Skills: • **discussing food tastes and differences between countries** Writing Skills: • **expressing your opinions about eating**	Words related to food and senses Words related to countries

WARM UP: Talk about it

Work with a partner and answer the questions below.

1. What is your favorite kind of ethnic food?
2. Is there a restaurant you like in particular? Why?

VOCABULARY: Matching

Match the words and phrases (1-8) and their definitions (a-h).

1. flavors	____	a. food prepared at home rather than a shop or restaurant
2. spices	____	b. a native of the country of Iran
3. home-made	____	c. the flavor in your mouth from food or drink
4. taste	____	d. dried plants used to make food spicier or sweeter
5. nationality	____	e. the special tastes a food has
6. West Indian	____	f. a native of any of the islands of the West Indies
7. Iranian	____	g. being a citizen of the country you were born in
8. culture	____	h. the ideas, customs and social behavior of a society

VIDEO: Before Watching

The Food Game

Make teams. Your teacher will call out a letter. You must write one item per category for that letter. The first person to fill out all the categories raises their hand. The person reads their answers out to the class and the students decide if they are all correct. If correct, the student wins a point for their team.

fruit	vegetable	dairy	bread	drink	dessert

VIDEO: While Watching

Activity 1:

What job do Sally and Jennifer have? Write your guess and then watch the video to check your answer.

Activity 2:

Write down all the nationalities you hear mentioned in the video. Then try to find them on a map.

VIDEO: After Watching

Design a West Indian meal. Write an ingredient in each section of the plate and describe how it is cooked. You can add more sections by drawing additional lines.

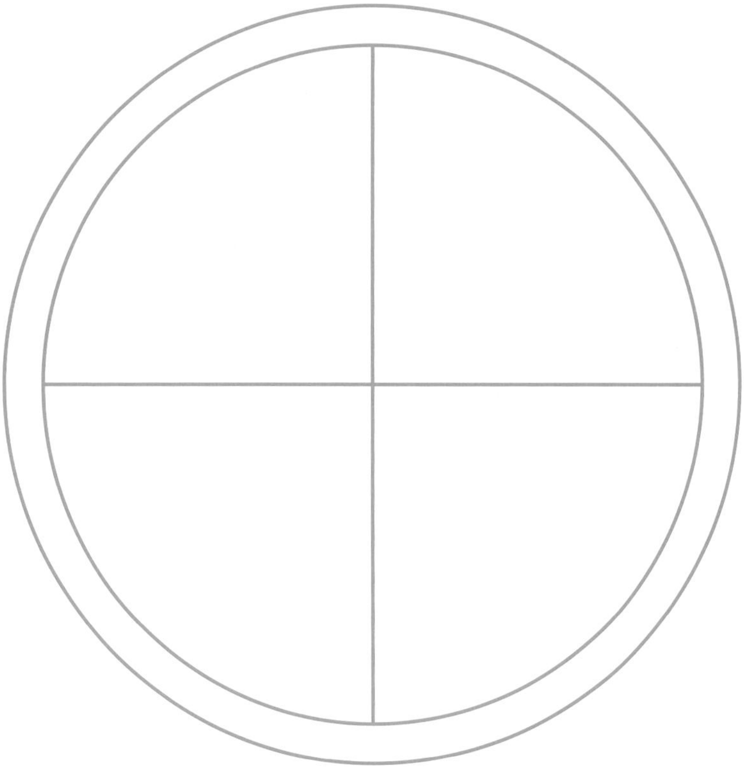

DISCUSSION

Make a small group and discuss the following question:

Do you think food brings people together? Why or why not?

WRITING: Critical Thinking

Think about the various times you have eaten together with other people, either at home or out at a restaurant. For you, do you think eating is a social experience? Explain your opinion giving a few examples.

QUOTABLE QUOTES:

"One cannot think well, love well, sleep well, if not has not dined well."

By Virginia Woolf

Look at the quote above. Think about this unit. What do you think the quote means?

VOICE DICTION: Video Shadowing

Start the video at 0:27 and play.

1. Fill in the blank with the missing words.

   They have a (   ) in Peckham where they (   ) West Indian food.

2. Watch the scene and pronounce at the same time. Repeat several times until you can do it smoothly.

CRITICAL DISCUSSION

Make groups of 3-4 students. Read each essay one by one. Then ...

- Choose the essay(s) with the most interesting ideas.
- Prepare to present those to the class in English.

WRITING

Work with a partner and design a short survey related to food (for example, eating habits, foods people have tried or least favorite foods). Make at least 5 questions. Then write up the survey, give it to your classmates and report the results.

OPTIONAL PROJECTS: Individual and Group

In groups of three, research past eating habits in Japan or a different culture of your choice. Then, they create a timeline that documents changes in eating habits up to the present. Try to predict future eating habits and include them in the timeline. You can use the timeline chart below to help you.

CEFR GOALS SELF- EVALUATION	
I can discuss food tastes from different countries	1---2---3---4---5
I can write my opinion about eating	1---2---3---4---5
I can understand words related to food and senses	1---2---3---4---5
I can understand and use words related to countries	1---2---3---4---5

Unit 11
Super Street Art
<Art>

Learning Goals	Vocabulary from the Video
Speaking Skills: • **discussing art** Writing Skills: • **political poster**	Words related to art Words related to fame

WARM UP: Talk about it

Work with a partner and answer the questions below.

1. Is there any interesting street art in your city or near where you live?
2. Do you think street art is a good or bad thing for the community? Why?

VOCABULARY: Matching

Match the words and phrases (1-8) and their definitions (a-h).

1. vandalism ____	a. to keep someone or something safe from injury or damage
2. protect ____	b. drawings and writings made in public places
3. celebrity ____	c. someone who is well-known or famous, especially in the entertainment business
4. mural ____	d. the crime of purposely damaging the property of others
5. gallery ____	e. a place that does not have a roof, or an event that takes place outside
6. open-air ____	f. a person who draws pictures for books, comics, magazines or newspapers
7. graffiti ____	g. a place that is used for showing works of art, sometimes so that they can be sold
8. illustrator ____	h. a very large picture that has been painted on the wall of a room or building

VIDEO: Before Watching

The Landmark Game

Work with a partner. Choose a picture from your phone of a nearby landmark (or just imagine it). Describe the image/place and see if your partner can guess it. Then switch roles.

VIDEO: While Watching

Activity 1:

Watch the video about street art in Bristol. Which mural is your favorite? Why? Would you like to go on a graffiti sightseeing tour in Bristol?

Activity 2:

Complete the sentences, then watch again and check.

1. A lot of people think street art isn't art, it's ______________________.
2. Bristol became famous for its street art because of ______________________.
3. Street art is part of Bristol's ______________________.
4. Before painting, street artists ______________________.
5. Street art always changes because ______________________.

VIDEO: After Watching

Debate: "Is graffiti art or vandalism?"

Divide the class into two teams. one team should argue that graffiti is art, and the other team should argue it is vandalism. You have 10 minutes to come up with three convincing ideas to support your theory. You may use the internet if necessary.

1. ______________________.
2. ______________________.
3. ______________________.

Take turns. One person from the first team must speak for at least 30 second. The other team should discuss how to respond. Go back and forth several times.

Use this space to take notes about what the other team says.

____

____

____

____

____

____

____

____

____

____

When you are finished, have a group discussion about your real opinions on this topic.

DISCUSSION

Make a small group and discuss the following question:

Do you think graffiti is really art? Why or why not?

WRITING: Critical Thinking

Situation: The city council is inviting citizens to come up with solutions to the graffiti problem and collect signatures. The most popular policy will become local law.

Task: In small groups, discuss what your ideal policy would be and produce a poster to promote it. Some ideas may include: graffiti being totally banned, always allowed, only permitted if it meets certain criteria or allowed for a limited amount of time.

Political posters usually have catchy titles; paragraph headings are in large font and are informative, paragraphs are short and clear, and there is usually a slogan at the end.

When you are finished, stick your poster to the walls and go around the class, reading the others and putting your signatures next to the ones they agree with. The poster with the most signature wins.

QUOTABLE QUOTES:

"Few people go to art exhibitions, these days the art comes to them!"

By Chris Geiger

Look at the quote above. Think about this unit. What do you think the quote means?

VOICE DICTION: Video Shadowing

Start the video at 0:58 and play.

1. Fill in the blank with the missing words.

   Now, street (　　　　　　) are an important (　　　　　) of the city's culture and (　　　　　).

2. Watch the scene and pronounce at the same time. Repeat several times until you can do it smoothly.

CRITICAL DISCUSSION

Make groups of 3-4 students. Read each essay one by one. Then ...

- Choose the essay(s) with the most interesting ideas.
- Prepare to present those to the class in English.

WRITING

Think about the different ways street art might impact a local community and then write a short essay about your ideas. Put your finished essay on your desk and then walk around the room and read some of the other essays.

OPTIONAL PROJECTS: Individual and Group

In groups of three, research popular street artists in Japan. Discuss the various artists and work together to choose one artist you like the best. Brainstorm a list of questions you might want to ask the artist about themselves and the artwork you chose (prepare a copy of this artwork). For example, ask about their early life, their studies, their inspiration, their technique etc. Each person in the group should research about 1 question so that you can answer the question if asked.

Next, put up the copy of the artwork on a wall and imagine it is an art gallery. One person from your group should impersonate the artist and try to answer questions from other students as if they were the artist.

CEFR GOALS SELF- EVALUATION	
I can discuss art.	1---2---3---4---5
I can write a political poster.	1---2---3---4---5
I can understand words related to art.	1---2---3---4---5
I can understand and use words related to fame.	1---2---3---4---5

Unit 12

Two Very Different Brothers <Family>

Learning Goals	Vocabulary from the Video
Speaking Skills: ● **discussing family** Writing Skills: ● **writing a survival guide**	Words related to jobs Words related to relationships

WARM UP: Talk about it

Work with a partner and answer the questions below.

1. Do you have any brothers or sisters? If so, tell your partner about them.
2. Do you think most brothers and sisters are close? Why or why not?

VOCABULARY: Matching

Match the words and phrases (1-8) and their definitions (a-h).

1. millionaire	____	a. to understand the full worth of something
2. politician	____	b. a person who has more than 1 million dollars or pounds
3. builder	____	c. to be worried or nervous about something
4. barista	____	d. a person who is professionally involved in politics
5. anxious	____	e. a person who makes something by putting parts together
6. reunion	____	f. feeling pleasure at a person's achievements
7. appreciate	____	g. when 2 or more people get together after a long separation
8. proud	____	h. a person who makes and serves coffee in a bar

VIDEO: Before Watching

Work in pairs and discuss the following questions:

Who are the most important people in your life? Why?

Then share your ideas with the class. List up key vocabulary related to family relationships and friendships.

VIDEO: While Watching

Activity 1:

You are going to watch a short documentary video called "Two Very Different Brothers". While you watch, think about the following 2 questions:

1. Why do you think the brothers decided to participate in this documentary?
2. Do you think participating in the documentary helped them?

Activity 2:

Watch the video again and make notes on how you think the brothers were feeling at different times in the video.

Before Meeting	
At Ivan's Event	
At The Exhibition	

VIDEO: After Watching

The video is part of a longer documentary about the relationship of the two brothers. With a partner, plan an interview with each of the brothers that could be included in the film.

When you are finished, compare your ideas and questions with another pair.

DISCUSSION

Work in small groups. Listen to the following parts of the video again and decide whether you think the speaker is being positive or negative about the other brother.

01:42 - 01:47: "I think it's quite glamorous really having a hippy brother to be honest. With his little beard and his scruffy hair ..."

02:42 - 02:52: "I just feel as if we have been brothers for a little bit, he's really kind of let me in and I really appreciate that. I just feel as if we've had a little bit of fun tonight".

02:54 - 03:03: "I've had the best evening with David, I really do enjoy seeing him, and I feel ... both love and also I'm proud of him."

Next, share your answers with the class and discuss the key language from the sections which suggest a positive/negative outlook.

WRITING: Critical Thinking

Do you think it is important to have a close relationship with your family? Discuss the topic in groups and then write an essay on your own that summarized the ideas you discussed and the feelings you have on this subject.

QUOTABLE QUOTES:

"Family is not an important thing,

it's everything."

By Michael J. Fox

Look at the quote above. Think about this unit. What do you think the quote means?

VOICE DICTION: Video Shadowing

Start the video at 1:02 and play.

1. Fill in the blank with the missing words.

   I must admit I'm quite (   ). I'm (   ) as well, but (   ).

2. Watch the scene and pronounce at the same time. Repeat several times until you can do it smoothly.

CRITICAL DISCUSSION

Make groups of 3-4 students. Read each essay one by one. Then ...

- Choose the essay(s) with the most interesting ideas.
- Prepare to present those to the class in English.

WRITING

Create a personality profile for two people in your family or close circle of friends. Interview each of them and create a report that explores their personalities and how their similarities and differences affect their relationship.

OPTIONAL PROJECTS: Individual and Group

Work with a small group. Imagine you've been asked by a teen magazine to write a "survival guide" for getting along with your family. Search the internet and look for entertaining examples, then read through and discuss them with your group. Next, work together to create your own family survival guide pamphlet. It should include:

- Advice and tips for getting along with your family (dos and don'ts)
- How to deal with common family problems
- Illustrations or images of some kind

Remember the audience is teenagers so try to make it as funny and entertaining as possible.

Finally, read each other's pamphlets and do an anonymous vote on the one you think the magazine should publish.

CEFR GOALS SELF- EVALUATION	
I can discuss family.	1---2---3---4---5
I can write a survival guide.	1---2---3---4---5
I can understand words related to relationships.	1---2---3---4---5
I can understand and use words related to jobs.	1---2---3---4---5

Unit 13
A Cool Job <Jobs>

Learning Goals	Vocabulary from the Video
Speaking Skills: ● **planning a commercial** Writing Skills: ● **arguing a point of view**	Words related to commercials Words related to ice sculpting

WARM UP: Talk about it

Work with a partner and answer the questions below.

1. Have you ever seen an ice sculpture before? What did you think?
2. Have you seen someone making an ice sculpture?

VOCABULARY: Matching

Match the words and phrases (1-8) and their definitions (a-h).

1. fragile ____ a. a TV or radio advertisement
2. luxury ____ b. very cold
3. freezing ____ c. an expensive item that is not really necessary
4. sculpture ____ d. a group of people who produces a movie or commercial
5. original ____ e. easily broken or damaged
6. go viral ____ f. to spread quickly and widely on the internet
7. commercial ____ g. being the first made, throught or performed
8. film crew ____ h. work of art made by cutting stone, wood or ice

VIDEO: Before Watching

The Water Game

Make several groups. Each group is a team.

In your group, quickly make a list of all the things water can be used for. Then take turns saying your ideas to the class. Teams get one point for every original idea they come up with.

VIDEO: While Watching

Activity 1:

What do you know about ice sculpting? Watch the video and complete the spider diagram with all the things you learned.

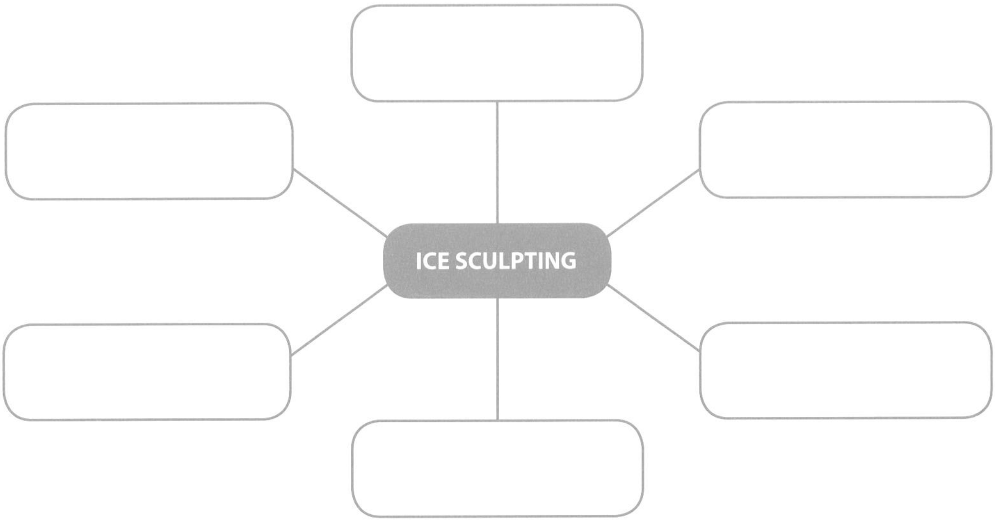

Activity 2:

Watch the video again. Then read the questions below and choose the best answer, a or b.

1. An event organizer might think ...
   a. We should have an ice sculpture, they're cool.
   b. We shouldn't have an ice sculpture, they're a waste of money.

2. Every day, Jack thinks ...
   a. I hate the cold.
   b. I have no problem with the cold.

3. The marketing manager thought ...
   a. Let's make a unique video, and people will share it online.
   b. Let's make an interesting TV commercial.

4. When the wheel broke, Jack thought ...
   a. That's it, I'm going home.
   b. OK, let's shoot without it.

5. The film crew thought ...
   a. We did a good job!
   b. We did a terrible job!

6. At the end, Jack thought ...
   a. I'm happy I did this.
   b. This was a waste of time.

VIDEO: After Watching

Natural Speech

Work in groups. You are going to design a commercial featuring an object made of ice. Discuss the following questions:

1. What the commercial is for
2. What the ice object will be
3. What happens in the commercial
4. Why it will be cool

Present your idea to the rest of the class.

DISCUSSION

Make a small group and discuss the following questions.

Do you think that ice sculpture is really art? Why or why not?

WRITING: Critical Thinking

"Ice sculptures are a waste of money!"

1. Work with a partner and brainstorm arguments in favor and against this point of view:

   In favour: *There are better things to spend your money on ...*

   Against: *If you have the money, why not ...*

2. Read the essay title below and write your essay.

   "Some people think ice sculptures are an unnecessary luxury, and that the money would be better spent on other things. To what extent do you agree?"

QUOTABLE QUOTES:

"Creativity takes courage."

By Henri Matisse

Look at the quote above. Think about this unit. What do you think the quote means?

VOICE DICTION: Video Shadowing

Start the video at 1:31 and play.

1. Fill in the blank with the missing words.

   The car company (   ) if they make (   ) and original video, it might (   ) on social media.

2. Watch the scene and pronounce at the same time. Repeat several times until you can do it smoothly.

CRITICAL DISCUSSION

Make groups of 3-4 students. Read each essay one by one. Then ...

- Choose the essay(s) with the most interesting ideas.
- Prepare to present those to the class in English.

WRITING

The ice sculpture game

Find a picture of an ice sculpture you find interesting and write a description of it on a separate paper. Make a group of 5-6 people and place the pictures on the desk in front of you. Shuffle the descriptions. One person reads out the descriptions one by one, the others try to grab the right picture as quickly as possible. The person who has the most pictures at the end is the winner.

OPTIONAL PROJECTS: Individual and Group

In small groups, research facts about the history of ice trade, which started at the beginning of the 19th century with a man called Frederic Tudor, "the ice king."

Before that time, people didn't use ice at all, and didn't see a need for it. Think about what we use ice for now, and how people in the past might have done without it.

Each person researches about this individually and reports their findings to the group. As a group, choose the most interesting 5-6 facts and make a multiple-choice quiz for the rest of the class.

Swap quizzes with other groups, vote for the most interesting facts, and then decide if you want to do more research about those most interesting points.

CEFR GOALS SELF- EVALUATION	
I can plan a commercial.	1---2---3---4---5
I can argue a point of vide.	1---2---3---4---5
I can understand words related to commercials.	1---2---3---4---5
I can understand and use words related to ice sculpting.	1---2---3---4---5

Unit 14
How to Make Money and Travel Full-Time <Life>

Learning Goals	Vocabulary from the Video
Speaking Skills: ● **discussing life goals** Writing Skills: ● **designing a dream van**	Words related to work Words related to travel

WARM UP: Talk about it

Work with a partner and answer the questions below.

1. Would you like to have a job where you could work from the beach or from home?
2. What kinds of jobs do you think could be done outside the office?

VOCABULARY: Matching

Match the words and phrases (1-8) and their definitions (a-h).

1. income	_____	a. to achieve a goal, fame, wealth or social status
2. be successful	_____	b. a large vehicle you can sleep in
3. shop	_____	c. sites and apps that let users share content with each other
4. camper-van	_____	d. studying or working for the whole of each week
5. full-time	_____	e. to buy things at a store or online
6. filmmaking	_____	f. the art of taking pictures with a camera
7. social media	_____	g. money received on a regular basis for work done
8. photography	_____	h. the process of making a film, usually for the public to see

VIDEO: Before Watching

As a group, list up on the board various things that you like or enjoy doing.
Next, discuss in small groups and then as a class the following question:

"Could any of these also be a way of making money? How?"

VIDEO: While Watching

Activity 1:

Think about the following questions while you watch the video:

1. Where do Bee and Theo live?
2. What do Bee and Theo use the internet for?

Activity 2:

Watch the video again. Use the titles in the videos to fill in the first column and then use your own words to complete the 2nd column.

Ways of making money	Why they do it
1.	
2.	
3.	
4.	

VIDEO: After Watching

Natural Speech

Work in groups. Try to think of other ways that Bee and Theo could make money while they travel in their van or boat. Then discuss your ideas with other groups.

DISCUSSION

Make a small group and discuss the following questions.

1. Would you prefer to travel full time or live and work in one place?
2. What problems could there be with traveling all the time?

WRITING: Critical Thinking

Imagine what it would be like if you could do your job and career without ever going to an office. Write about the pros and cons of living your life in this way.

QUOTABLE QUOTES:

"Most fears that have to do with people working remotely come from a lack of trust."

By Jason Fried

Look at the quote above. Think about this unit. What do you think the quote means?

VOICE DICTION: Video Shadowing

Start the video at 0:32 and play.

1. Fill in the blank with the missing words.

   We started off (   ) camper-van and then got a (   ) as well.

2. Watch the scene and pronounce at the same time. Repeat several times until you can do it smoothly.

CRITICAL DISCUSSION

Make groups of 3-4 students. Read each essay one by one. Then ...

- Choose the essay(s) with the most interesting ideas.
- Prepare to present those to the class in English.

WRITING

Working in pairs, pretend you live in a van like Bee and Theo.

Your task is to plan, write and then record a 2-minute podcast about life in the van. The podcast should include:

- The benefits of living in a van
- The difficulties of living in a van
- A trip you enjoyed
- Your future plans

Then listen to all the podcasts and vote for the one that is best. If voice recorders are not available, you can perform the podcast for the class.

OPTIONAL PROJECTS: Individual and Group

Work in a group and design a van you would like to live in. Think about what difficulties you will need to overcome living in a van and think of exciting design features. Write and draw this up and then present your design to the rest of the class and hold a vote for the best van.

CEFR GOALS SELF- EVALUATION	
I can discuss about life goals.	1---2---3---4---5
I can design and write about a dream van.	1---2---3---4---5
I can understand words related to work.	1---2---3---4---5
I can understand and use words related to travel.	1---2---3---4---5

NOTE

NOTE

Expanding Horizons: [B-921]
Critical Thinking through Authentic Video〈CEFR A2-B1〉
世界を巡る映像で学ぶ総合英語〈準中級〉

1 刷 2021 年 2 月 16 日
2 刷 2024 年 3 月 29 日

著 者 チャールズ ブラウン Charles Brown
田邉祐司 Yuji Tanabe

発行者 南雲一範 Kazunori Nagumo
発行所 株式会社 南雲堂
〒162-0801 東京都新宿区山吹町 361
NAN'UN-DO Co., Ltd.
361 Yamabuki-cho, Shinjuku-ku, Tokyo 162-0801, Japan
振替口座：00160-0-46863
TEL: 03-3268-2311（営業部：学校関係）
03-3268-2384（営業部：書店関係）
03-3268-2387（編集部）
FAX: 03-3269-2486

編集者 加藤 敦
装 丁 銀月堂
組 版 Office haru
検 印 省 略
コード ISBN978-4-523-17921-4 C0082

Printed in Japan

E-mail nanundo@post.email.ne.jp
URL https://www.nanun-do.co.jp/